**The Mental Locker**

Author: Tim Dixon

Printed in the United States of America

Available on Amazon.com, CreateSpace, and TheMentalLocker.com

ISBN: 1519386699
ISBN-13: 978-1519386694

# ACKNOWLEDGMENTS

My vision for *The Mental Locker* is to give people some simple tools to improve their lives — permission to play a bigger game in whatever arena they exist. If you are looking for something that is formally edited and properly formatted, this might not be the book for you. This is just me, edited by a good friend who gets who I am. As you continue to read, it is my hope that you simply get lost in the conversation.

There are so many people to thank and I will not attempt to name everyone. I have been blessed to be surrounded by so many people better than myself. It forced me to be successful. I had to try to keep up! For this project, a huge thanks to China McCarney and Matt Morse, two amazing men who see life through a similar lens. Thanks, guys!

My parents, Les and Bev, and big sis Kim have had such a huge impact on who I am, and they are always near my heart for that unwavering support. You are the best and you will see yourself in the words to follow.

To my amazing wife Kendra and two kids, Hailey and Brayden, I say thank you for putting up with me for so many years as I chased my dreams. I am done running and now it is time for me to clear the path for your dreams. All I want is for you to read this and get excited about creating your plan to take over the world. I love you to the moon and back!

# FOREWORD
*By China McCarney*

Everyone wants to improve. Everyone wants to be a better version of himself or herself. We all want to see better results but don't always know where to turn or what steps we should implement. You are clearly one of these people because you have picked up this book and are looking for answers on how to improve. This book is not going to help you be a better version of yourself; it will help you become the BEST version of yourself.

This concept of being the best version of yourself was introduced to me by Tim Dixon some time ago. I had not been around Tim that much but was fortunate enough to hear him speak at Cal State Fullerton, his alma mater, where he was undefeated on the mound and won a National Championship – that gives you a small insight into his character and work ethic. I heard him give one speech and was immediately hooked. We all have certain people and experiences in life that don't leave us. They are the most vivid in our memory bank and are special to us. That is the type of recollection I have when I think of my first encounter with Mr. Dixon and his energy and message.

The speech I heard was 45 minutes long, and to this day I often reference it as something that changed my life. He spoke of some concepts I had heard before, but he expressed them in an impactful way that made them realistic to implement – concepts like Amateur versus Professional, Being a Predator, Your Relationship with Practice and, of course, Being the Best Version of Yourself. I was "fired up," which is a term Tim uses often with the same passion and energy as he lives his life every day.

The greatest thing about Tim's teachings and concepts is that they are not a massive overhaul. It is not him up on a perch preaching down on how to achieve 100% success. It is about implementing small steps that build up over time to achieve greatness and to be elite. Tim lives the grind every day just like all of us. His uniqueness is that he thrives on the grind and he lives to help people embrace that grind and get better.

When he approached me to let me know that he would be writing this book, I couldn't help but get excited for every prospective reader that would have the pleasure of turning the pages of his words. He changed my perspective and approach to life in one speech and I could anticipate countless lives being impacted for the better by his books.

I could not be more honored to be involved in this project because Tim has impacted me significantly for the better. He has something very unique to offer every single person that makes the intelligent decision to listen or to read. Obviously, you are one of these people and you are in for a treat. You are on a journey to becoming the best version of yourself. Excellence is a choice and there is no doubt in my mind that Tim's words will help you get closer to being elite and being special.

Enjoy the grind!

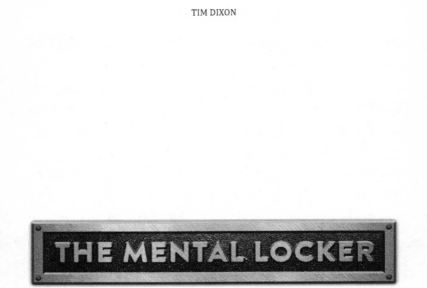

When I was thirteen years old, I had a dream of playing professional baseball. I had no idea on how to get there, but I knew I had to work. So that is what I did: I went to work and became obsessed with my dream.

Everything I did was for one reason and that was to fulfill that dream. I eliminated all options and put all my eggs in one basket. Ten years of pain, struggle, triumph and frustration paid off when I was drafted in the 14th round by the Montreal Expos in the 1995 Major League Amateur Draft.

Pretty much my whole career in baseball had been a mess leading up to that magical year in 1995. I had success but never fit in. I was told more times than I can count that I was not good enough. Fuel to my fire! As I got older things got worse. The talent surrounding me got better and everyone quickly caught up to me.

College was a nightmare! Four schools in four years, and leading up to my senior year that dream was looking like a shot in the dark. My senior year something magical happened. My work ethic did not change but something about this stop was different. The expectations finally met with mine. I found a bunch of ball players that were as obsessed as I was. More importantly, I learned how to use my mind as an asset, not a self-exploding dream crusher. When my mind caught up with my body, magic happened.

That team was 57-9 and we were crowned 1995 National Champions. I was 13-0 as the Saturday starting pitcher and still hold the record for the most wins without a loss at Fullerton. Insane! It was as if everything came together. The perfect storm. The stars aligned, and whatever corny saying you can insert here.

That team was inducted into the Cal State Fullerton Hall of Fame in October 2013. There is not a day that passes by when I do not think of that year and how it changed the course of my life. As we approached our twenty-year reunion, there was no coincidence that most members of that team have success in their lives. Some played in the Big Leagues and made millions of dollars; some coach, and others are very successful in the business world. All have one thing in common: Hard work is engrained in their molecules.

I played the game I love till the age of 30, and when I was done playing I began coaching. I spent thirteen years as a coach, eleven of them at the college level.

Walking away from coaching was the hardest decision I ever made. Baseball was my life – the only thing I knew – and now I was in the "real" world. What the hell was I going to do? I did the only thing I knew how to do, and I went to work.

Looking back at that dream of becoming a professional athlete, I now know that dream was temporary. My new dream is to become a professional at life. Taking everything I learned to achieve my first dream and apply it to my next. That same grind works in everything we do. Being the CEO of a Fortune 500 company or a stay-at-home mom requires ridiculous commitment to master that skill. If you are willing to work and are in it for the long haul, I will promise you one thing. You will not regret it. You will shatter every expectation of who you think you are and discover the BADASS within.

The ultimate result here is to be undefeated from the neck up. Your body will fail and you will encounter pain, but you have 100% control of your thoughts, so that is what we will focus on.

# WHAT IS YOUR PLAN?

---

Mental warriors, welcome to a new beginning, a fresh start, or just another push towards not who you are but who you were meant to be. Funny thing is you may not even know who that person is. That's OK. When you are done with this book, you will have a better idea, but the process of discovering the best you are will require more than these written words. I want to congratulate you on taking action to master your mental skills, whatever that might mean to you. It could be to simplify or for some to complicate. Getting complicated is not always a bad thing, and my vision for this book is to redefine words like *complicated, fear, anxiety, stress* and all these other so called "negatives" in our lives. If we look at the words with different lenses, then we see our world differently. We get to paint our own picture of what life looks like, not what others tell us it should look like.

There are a lot of current topics with the mental game, mental toughness, mental performance or whatever you want to call it, and its potential power. Why is *The Mental Locker* different? We are not reinventing the wheel here. The things we will be discussing are topics that have been talked about for hundreds of years. The difference here is these are real-life stories, not science. I love science but I want you to see, feel and hear about all the pain, struggle and work that get you to where you want to be. At the end of a study you get results. At the end of *The Mental Locker* you get tools to apply to your life that will give you the best chance for success in everything you do.

I understand results matter. Results get you the big payday. They can also get you fired and everything in between. I have experienced just about everything you can imagine. I have been in the grind. I have won a National Championship. I have been told I wasn't good enough at every level. I played professional baseball for six years and was released (fired) twice. I worked with some of the best in business and was laughed at by some of the best. I am one of you. I am not a placebo effect or a control group. I am a real live person in real life sharing my success, failures and stories of what has worked for me. I know the grind of what it takes to rise to the top, and it is possible for everyone. All walks of life can take *The Mental Locker* and apply it to anything they choose. Results are on you. Your work is on you. Your passion is on you. Your ability to never stop until you get what you want is on you. If this upsets you, then you should probably stop reading because there is no fluff here. This is real and not for everyone. Honestly, isn't that what you are looking for anyway? A raw experience giving you direction and not a quick fix? I don't believe in quick fixes. Most people want to go from point A to point B as quickly as they can. I call it a "microwave lifestyle" and if we don't get those results, we quit. It is the guts between points A and B that create the best memories – the sense of accomplishment in knowing that you gave all of yourself all of the time. Let's get to work.

For the past twenty-five years I have been haunted by the word *perfection*. I learned the hard way that perfection does not exist; however, the pursuit of perfection is what it takes to be THE BEST. My stories, my experiences, what's worked and my failures are mine. You may find yourself in my stories and learn from my mistakes, saving you time and pain. I love that but in a way I hate it. Why? In order to really discover who you are, you have to suffer, so I am not going to take away all your pain but possibly will make it a little softer.

Attack these words with an open mind and challenge yourself to get out of your comfort zone. Be honest with yourself and really listen to that voice within. It's the only voice that has a say in how you live your life. I am sure that voice has been ignored or second-guessed for some time. We all doubt and often let outside sources dictate our actions, so you are not alone. This is your journey, so kindly tell all the outside experts on your life to go to hell. You don't have to be kind. In fact, I prefer the gritty version.

Take action! You're going to get some great tools. You're going to get some tangible things, and if you apply them, you will get results. Not a fan of that word but I know it is important. So let's address this early so that we are clear on results and process. We all want results. I get it. Here is the question I want you to ask yourself when thinking about results: Who do I have to become to earn those results? Notice how I said *earn*, not *deserve*. I do not think anyone deserves anything. Greatness is never deserved; it's earned with blood, sweat, tears and amazing stories.

Goal Setting, and I use this phrase lightly. Most people think of goals as something you talk about on New Year's Eve and then go back to your habits and routine six weeks later. Goals are temporary but they are a good starting point. As I discuss this, keep in mind that this exercise is to determine where you will go – setting the foundation to accomplishing greatness. Once you clearly define your goals, you will turn them into your Declaration, just like the Declaration of Independence that was created in 1776. The men who wrote their names on that paper were willing to die for those words. Sound a little different than a goal? When that declaration is created, you will announce to the world whatever it is you will become. Attach those words to your molecules and then get to work becoming that person. I am starting with goals because I want you to get this right. Work out all the details during the goal-setting phase and get clear on exactly what you want. Those goals will give you direction. It's going to really set the foundation for the rest of the process. Once this is complete, you will embody the words you have written and begin a relationship with your future self. You must know your future self so you can get your current self prepared to become him or her with mind, body and soul.

I have broken goals into three categories: untouchable goals, commitment goals, and grinding goals.

**Untouchable goals** are your big, hairy, audacious dreams. When you're thinking about these goals, I want you to think big: owning your own business, being the best player in the world at your sport, or creator of the next Facebook. Do not put lids on your expectations. Dream as big as you want — there are no limits. These goals are five, ten or even twenty years out.

**Commitment goals** are going to be more tangible things like losing ten pounds in six months, gaining ten pounds in the weight room, learning how to eat better, or a new skill that will improve your game in what you do. These goals range from six months to a few years in length and are measureable.

**Grinding goals** are my favorite. They are the little things that you do on a daily basis to separate yourself from your competition. It is the attention to detail with your craft. It is the discipline to move forward every day no matter how little each step may be. It is redefining your relationship with practice.

All three levels are to be congruent with each other. Your big, huge, untouchable goals are what I want you to look at every once in a while.

We know they're there, but we're not necessarily focused on those daily.

Your commitment goals are results of accomplishing your grinding goals over a period of time, and the untouchable goals are what you see after accomplishing your commitment goals over a period of time. Each level flows right into the next until you look up one day and find that you have reached the unthinkable.

If you are questioning the reality of this, then you are the exact person I am writing this for. You have settled, and I want you to unleash your true potential and break away from thinking small. I love the quote by Henry Ford that states, *"Whether you think you can or cannot, you are right."*

Think bigger. Dream bigger and demand more from yourself. Play a bigger game!
When setting goals it is important to understand the difference between process- and outcome-oriented goals. *Outcome* is just another nasty word for *results*, and we know how I feel about

that word. We want to focus on the things you have 100% control over. Want an amazing outcome? Focus on what it takes to get it and plug away daily at the process. You will be amazed at what will appear when you take your mind off the outcome and focus on the process. Example: I want to lose ten pounds (outcome). In order for me to lose ten pounds, I have to eat right, exercise and educate myself on a healthy life style (process). In order to get the outcome, I must focus on the process. Confused? Let's simplify. To get results I have to determine what it takes to get it. Work backwards. Make sense?

When creating your goals, the more detailed you are the better. It's attention to detail. It's the little things done over a period of time that are going to give you your big goals and dreams.

We're going to talk a lot about your relationship with practice. We're going to talk a lot about loving the hate, because being the best is not easy. The most important thing that I want you to understand throughout this process of the Mental Locker is there is no finish line. To be the best of the best, it's never over. When you get to the top, you look for the next mountain to climb and you go until your heart explodes. Now that's living a good life.

My first Spring Training in 1996 was with the Montreal Expos. We shared our Spring Training Complex with the Atlanta Braves in West Palm Beach, Florida. One of my first experiences was watching Tom Glavine, Greg Maddux, John Smoltz and Steve Avery throw bullpens. At that time they were arguably the best rotation in the Big Leagues. I sat in the bullpen and I watched each one execute pitch after pitch with an effortless approach. First thought that came to my mind was, what in the hell am I doing here? Their ability to hit spots, repeat mechanics and adjust pitch to pitch was poetry in motion. Many would say that these men were gifted and blessed with the ability to throw a baseball at a world-class level. What most do not see was their relationship with practice. They worked harder than anyone and were committed to excellence in everything they did.

After Greg Maddux threw his bullpen, we stuck around and asked him some questions about his routine. "Hey, Mr. Maddux, how do you throw your change-up?" He looked at me and said, "You know, I'm currently working on a new one. I'm not quite sure yet." I'm thinking to myself, *This guy has won three Cy Young awards, he's won multiple Golden Gloves and is probably one of the best pitchers in the Big Leagues at the time, and he's working on a new change-up.* Mind blowing! But not really. As you begin to study the greats at whatever they do, they all have one thing in common: Their relationship with practice far exceeds the norm. The more I dive into this the more I am shocked about the simplicity of what it takes to rise to the top. It's hard and demands massive action, but it is all about the little things done over a period of time that create the best.

So I hate to tell you (actually I don't hate this at all – I LOVE IT), but the work is never done. It's a constant grind. You are always pushing boundaries to be the best. It's about your relationship with practice, and there is a good chance that you will get sick and tired of me saying *relationship with practice*. I will try to find other words to describe your daily practice, but it is a game changer and makes all the difference in the world.

You took the initiative to read *The Mental Locker* and give yourself that advantage over your competition. Now you have to hold yourself accountable. I want you to be as honest as you can with yourself, and I want you to be as detailed as you can as you read this book. Of course, I want this to be a book that is fun, but more importantly I want you to put this book down and take massive action to create the life you want and stop settling for less than AMAZING! The fun will come when you create a life worth living. Seeing amazing people shrink down to society's size makes me cringe.

I have some questions I want you to spend some time on. As you answer these, it will add layers to your clarity of where you want to go and how you are going to get there. This book is just like everything else in life. You will get out of it what you put into it.

Here are some questions to think about.

What is your end result? What do you want to get out of this book? What does your life look like in a world where EVERYTHING is possible?

What are your weaknesses? The things that are getting in the way of your best life?

What is your current relationship with practice? This can be applied to anything you do. What are you doing to separate yourself from your competition? You have to be honest with yourself in this question and you have to give some details.

What are your untouchable goals? Your big, big goals? Ten to twenty years from now what does your life look like?

What are your commitment goals? What are some of the things that are a few months out that you want to accomplish? Remember, we want process, not results.

What are your grinding goals? What are the things that you're going to do on a daily basis that will allow you to achieve your commitment goals?

What are some action steps that you can take now to apply to the above questions? Answering these questions will give you a good foundation on what you want to accomplish.

What's going to be the process and what are some things you can apply right now? Remember, this is all about massive action. Here's some information, here are some tools, and here are some techniques. Now what are you going to do with them?

You've identified your goals and in time will turn them into your declaration. You have clarity on what that looks like down to the last detail. Now it is time to create that vision. What do those words look like? Paint, draw or sculpt something that brings this to life.

A vision board is great! Find pictures that identify with your vision, then put the board where you see it several times a day. Quotes, poems, songs, sentences on cue cards or creative ways you can be reminded of your path – place these reminders everywhere, such as your bathroom, car, work, school or phone. Very important to make sure these triggers are present in your vulnerable environments. That's where you need the push the most, so give yourself the ammunition to fight your distractions.

Now we need to work on our biggest and best tool. The brain – the most important ally in this fight. It will guide you to everything or destroy you. Best thing is you have 100% control of how you think, act and react, so that is why we are spending our time with the details of how we think.

# POWER OF PERCEPTION

---

The power of perception... What does that mean? The mind doesn't know the difference between perception and reality. What you think about and what you believe are your reality. If you have the mindset that you're a victim, that the world is against you, and there are constant negative thoughts, that's going to be your reality. We have all been around people who are never happy. I call them energy vampires. They suck the life out of you. They have no chance at success. They can't see the good in anything.

We have also been around people who have an amazing presence. Something about them draws you in. They walk into the room and everyone senses security and attraction. They don't have to say a word and you connect with them. They have the best outlook on life and create an energy that is hard to explain.

You can put these two individuals in the same situation and be blown away by how each describes it. Negative Norm (or Nancy) is complaining how hard something is and how he (or she) never gets a break while Positive Paul (or Pam) accepts the circumstances as a challenge and a moment of growth. I know who I want to be around!

NN sits back and waits for an opportunity. PP (I laughed a little) creates his or her opportunities. Bad runs *from* fear. Good runs *towards* fear. I can go on for hours but you get the point. The crazy thing is that this is all choice. I ask myself, who would choose to be miserable?

I have come up with an answer that gives these numb individuals the benefit of the doubt. Habits. You see this from generation to generation where people live their lives based on their environment. You grow up in a negative environment; those are habits you create. It goes for the positive as well. "The apple doesn't fall far from the tree" is spot on. The biggest mistake is we feel we are stuck and "it is what it is." By the way, I hate that saying. It is what you make it. Don't like your current situation; change it. All Choice.

None of this is "God given" or genetics. It has everything to do with the environment you put yourself in and the choices you make. Yes, I repeated myself because this is so important. If you cannot get past this point, then the rest of the process will be a challenge. Stop blaming others for where you are – grab hold of your life and CHOOSE to make the necessary changes.

More times than not we set ourselves up for failure. We talk ourselves out of success before we even start. It seems crazy that we are our worst enemy, but I have seen time after time amazing people squash themselves or reduce themselves to fit in. I have no interest in fitting in, and if you do, you will be temporary. We are not looking for Temporary; we are looking for Legendary!

It goes back to your perception. How do you perceive yourself? Do you hope you have success or do you know you're going to have success? I love the quote, "Thoughts are things. Beliefs make them so." We have all these great thoughts but you've got to believe them. When I mean believe them, I mean in the fibers of your soul you've got to believe you're the best.

You have to have the mindset that you are the best. You have to be your biggest ally as opposed to your worst enemy. A lot of times we are our own worst enemy. We get in our way of success. We put lids on our expectations and put boundaries on our limits before we even try: "Well, no, no, no, I can't do that." We tell ourselves if we can or cannot do something before we even attempt it. If you get out of your way, your body is going to instinctively do what it's supposed to do or what it's taught to do, and it goes back to your relationship with practice.

What are you thinking about? What's your perception? How are you going about your daily business? What's your mindset going into practice? Are you doing it just to do it, or are you doing it with purpose like no other? With the passion and purpose knowing you are separating yourself from your competition no matter the arena?

The right perception will shatter your expectations of what you think you're capable of doing. It's going to allow you to reach your untouchable goals and your commitment goals, and it will give you the energy to constantly grind through those goals on a daily basis. That's what it's all about; it's doing the little things, the small details, over a period of time. Slowly those goals turn into your declaration and you are unstoppable!

You're going to hear me say that a lot, but that's what it takes to be successful. Mastering the basic fundamentals takes approximately 10,000 hours. How do we accelerate the process? Some say you can't, but I think you can. When we become obsessed with the best and our body physically and emotionally changes, those 10,000 hours come quicker. Most never get there because they are not fully committed. They bounce back from option to option, never accomplishing anything. Find your passion, throw away options B, C and D, and don't stop until you get what you want.

One of the basics is your perception. How do you perceive yourself as an athlete, businessman/woman or a person? When you look in the mirror, do you like what is staring back at you? Look deep into your eyes and ask yourself if THE BEST is hiding in there begging to come out and play. Letting him or her out is scary because of the unknown, but when you give yourself that freedom, you better be ready to have everything you have ever wanted. Not being ready and seeing greatness often scares people and they immediately shrink back to mediocrity. I don't understand this.

Unleashing the beast is a process. He or she doesn't just come and go. It has to be given permission and there is a lot of courage involved. When the perception of everyday life changes for the good, things start to shift and the world starts preparing you for what's to come. That is a life designed to give you and everyone that surrounds you everything!

So about your perception of reality: How are you thinking about things? What are your thoughts? Do you believe in yourself? Do you have doubts in yourself? Are you getting in your own way?

Once you start thinking about that and as you go about it, you're going to have a thought, you're going to have an emotion, and you need to ask yourself, *Is this working for me or is this working against me?* There is no in-between; it's either helping you or hurting you.

Just thinking about it alone, you will make more decisions that help you rather than hurt you. You know what? You're not always going to make the right decision, but how do you handle failure? Failure is a part of the learning curve. *Okay, I failed at this situation. Why did I fail and how can I do it better next time*? Boom – move forward, don't dwell on it.

Did you know on average it takes seven times to hear one thing before you take action? As you start recognizing me repeating things of importance, it will begin to register more. Does it always take seven times? Nope. Sometimes it's one, and for some reason it smacks you across the face and once you hear it, you can't get it out of your mind. Those are great moments that need to be celebrated. Some call them "ah-ha" moments. I call them awareness moments. The words line up with what you need at that moment, and if you are paying attention, they grab hold of you and won't let go. Look for those moments in your daily life and they will surface. They have been there the whole time waiting for you to be there.

Let's do some work. The questions below will dig a little deeper on the topic of perception. When chewing on these, be as detailed as possible.

What is your personal definition of The Power of Perception? Don't look it up. Trust your experience to come up with the answer.

Think of some examples on how your perception in any given situation has created failure... Examples of when your perception led you to success or kept you optimistic in a tough situation. We have all been there. We go into a situation fired up to be great at it. Something happens and it blows up in your face. Other times where a situation you perceive to be negative turns into a great experience. An example of each kind of moment would be great.

What are some things that you can apply immediately on how you perceive your environment? Thoughts that get you over the hump, get you through that adversity or pressure?

Have there been times when you sensed the shift of your perception from optimistic to negative? Once you recall a situation, try to pinpoint what shifted the positive to the negative. As we identify those moments, we may recognize them as a pattern. Once we identify the pattern, we can be aware of when it happens and make the necessary change to deliver a better outcome.

List some specific action steps on how you will put yourself in the best situation possible no matter the circumstance, based on your perception.

You have to believe to achieve. You have to know in your heart of hearts that you are the best. I want you to say to yourself, "I give myself permission to fail." Say it. Say it loud and with conviction. Go on. If you have to hide somewhere to do it, then get up and find that space. Feels good, doesn't it? It gives you freedom. Freedom to explore the unknown.

Good work. I can see the change already. I really can't see through the book, but I bet you feel some changes happening. If not, revisit what you are taking action on. Yeah, it's OK – let it happen and celebrate those little victories. From this moment forward, look for those moments you can celebrate. Doing this gives you that energy to continue the journey.

# CONTROLLING THE CONTROLLABLES

Let's touch on perception real quick before we move on. As you read each chapter you will see the progression of this process. There is a method to the madness. You have created goals that will become your declaration. After talking about perception, you are starting the process of putting yourself in a good frame of mind. That frame of mind will allow you to grind through the day with one thing on your mind: being the best!

Approach everything you do with the same significance. We tend to label situations as important or not important. A job interview is very important, so we prepare for that. Eye contact with a stranger is not important. Imagine a life where everything matters. Everything has the same significance. That's living a good life.

Let's get to Controlling the Controllables. This is a big one. There is so much that we cannot control in life. When we eliminate all the crap, we now have more energy to focus on the things that matter. Unfortunately, a lot of results in life come from the things we cannot control. This is where it gets tricky. We are surrounded by a results-oriented society, yet most of the time we cannot control the result. We can control giving ourselves the best chance for results, but that is about it.

So, what can we control if we can't control the results? It's funny, but when I ask this question, most people think they can control the results until we dive a little deeper. A few minutes into the conversation, just about every time, there is a moment of recognition that they have wasted a lot of time and energy on something they could not control.

Back to the question. If we can't control the results, how can we be successful? The process. The process. The process. I will reframe from writing that four more times to let it sink in. Remember it takes an average of seven times for someone to take action. The process.

You want results. We all want results. I get it. We want to win and be successful. How do you get the result? What do you have to do to get the result you want? That is the process.

Here is the beauty of this. I know you want results. Now we are going to focus on what we can control to get those results, and that is the process. You have 100% control of the process (I think that may be seven times?) and that is your focus. Identify what you want (results) and determine what it takes to get what you want (process), then get to work and don't stop until you get it. Simple, right? NO!

There are a lot of factors that come into play when you are put into pressure situations. Most people fear them. Some crumble during them. Some thrive. In my experience the one thing that always factors in the downward spiral is your emotions. When you make emotional decisions, then regret, frustration, anger and other negatives typically follow. When we see someone who thrives in the high-pressure moments, we admire him or her. We think of them as "gifted" and often think *I wish I could do that*. You can. The only difference between you and the superstar is that their relationship with practice is better than yours.

Of course you have to have talent to be a superstar, but define talent. Nowhere in the definition does it talk about passion, purpose and heart to be the best. Talent will only get you so far. What are you going to do after that? If you rely on just talent, you are temporary. Not interested. When you see talent paired with an undeniable relationship with practice, you are witnessing legendary. I want that! Find your talents. If you don't compare with other talents, you write the script for you and no one else.

What are some things that you are allowing to consume you, yet you don't have control over? You're going to find as you think about this that most of your energy is wasted on the things you cannot control. They suck the life out of you and leave you feeling lost at times. If you are not making progress on something in your life right now, ask yourself one question: Can I control this? Chances are you cannot.

As I stand on my soapbox for a moment, let me tell you why I think so many people struggle to get through everyday life. They are not present. We humans tend to spend most of our time thinking about what has happened or what will happen instead of what is happening. Dwelling on the mistakes that we have made and dreaming of a better future. We consume ourselves with the thought that something better will come along with everything. *The grass is greener on the other side* is a saying that destroys our chances of being happy. Don't get me wrong; I feel you should always be pushing the boundaries and striving for greatness, but with a sense of gratitude for what you have and a level of respect for the journey you are on. Instead of complaining about the things you do not have, be grateful for the things you do have. When you shift your thoughts to that, you become present. What do we have 100% control of? Now! That's it, nothing else. Control now and it opens the doors to amazing opportunities.

Start thinking about what you have the ability to control. Start locking in on those few things and you're going to see a shift in your focus. That attention to detail is really going to start moving you in the direction of creating your best life.

When you get out of your way and eliminate all the factors you cannot control, it gets easier. Not easy, but easier. Controlling the situation or controlling how you handle the situation gives you power. If you can't control it, that moment does not deserve your energy. Save that energy for being awesome!

Before we dive into some questions, I want to make sure you have put some thought into this. Have you thought about what you have 100% control over? Put yourself in any recent situation you have been in and determine what you actually could have controlled. My guess is less than five things for any scenario you mustered up. For me, it sounds a heck of a lot easier to lock in on three to five things instead of countless things you can't control. Not to mention they suck the life out of you! Energy vampires!

You know the drill. When you answer the question, be real with yourself. The more detailed the better. It may be tough but the more clarity you get, the better you become on the other side. It is important that you ask yourself those tough questions, but make sure you give yourself honest answers.

Think of a recent moment in your life where you experienced failure of any kind. Be detailed. What was the outcome? How did it make you feel? As you go back and relive some moments, make sure you are not judging yourself. See this as a way to help prepare you for future situations and possibly even the same situation. This is not a beat-down session. This is an awakening moment. That's all.

Re-create that experience only focusing on the few things you can control.

Here's why we do this. I would go back after a performance or a moment that did not have the outcome I desired. I would write down some details and then re-create that same situation with the desired outcome or handling it based on what I had control over.

I want to be clear that we are not going to eliminate all failure that occurs in life or manipulate everything to always go our way. That's not the point. I want you to go back and relive some situation only to see if you let the uncontrollable get to you. If you did, relive it focusing on what you can control.

Now think of some strategies that give you clarity on what you have the ability to control. This is harder than I am making it sound – I understand that. I also want you to understand that this will not happen overnight. It will take time, but the shift begins when you start asking yourself the simple question, "Can I control this?" This gets thrown out of the window when emotions are involved. Someone hurts you or a loved one. Someone pissed you off, challenged who you are, and the list goes on. How do you handle it? Most of the time we react and try to defend. Most of the time it does not end well. Emotional moments are hard; I understand. Best advice I can give you is to try to put a gap between the moment and the reaction. If you can just take ONE deep breath, it can be enough for you to react a different way. Sometimes it doesn't matter what you do. Evaluate, adjust and move on. Don't let it stop you from where you are going.

List some details you have 100% control over. Get specific. The smallest detail matters. For me it always comes back to how I handle a situation. I am an emotional guy and tend to react very quickly with no compassion. It is a daily grind for me and I am working on it. It is getting better but I still have work to do. As soon as I could admit that's who I was, that's when I was able to start working on it. Until you are honest with yourself, you will never reach your maximum potential. You can fool everyone around you, but you cannot fool yourself. Stop going external for answers and start going internal.

As you eliminate the things you can't control, how does that change your approach to any situation? Now that you've gotten rid of all the garbage, getting rid of all the stuff that you can't control, what changes? OK, honestly, are you ever going to get rid of the garbage? NO! We can eliminate a lot of it — but failure, negative people, and emotional situations are never going away. It goes back to perception. Change how you see these moments. They are here to help you grow. It challenges you to see how badly you want something. We all love a good challenge — so go get it!

Controlling what you can control sounds easy, but this may be one of the hardest things to master. I don't think this work ever stops. When emotions are involved, it is easy to get sucked into the moment. We have addressed this already, but it is important to remind yourself. This takes practice and you will fail. Key is to start the process of paying attention to what you can control. When you get into a situation, ask yourself, *Can I or can I not control this?* If you answer *yes*, take charge and commit to that moment. If you cannot, ask what you can control and focus on that. As emotions rise, think of them as a wave that comes and goes. An emotion typically lasts no longer than 90 seconds. When it comes, acknowledge it, let it surface and let it go away. Try to avoid reaction until the emotion has passed. It will help you make better choices. If the emotion gets the best of you, learn from it and move on. The more you practice, the better you get.

I live near the ocean and when I heard Dr. Joan Rosenburg talk about emotions as waves, it really resonated with me. That might resonate with you as well, but if it doesn't, find something that does. Instead of a wave, maybe it is verse of a song, or something in nature that you connect with. Think of it as a buffer between the moment and the reaction to that moment.

# ROUTINE

_____

Throughout high school and college, and even as a professional, there were certain things I did every time I pitched. After each pitch, I would immediately wipe the dirt area where my foot would land and work my way to the rubber. Once that rubber was clean I would step up, get the sign, take a deep breath and deliver. This was the most consistent thing I had – my routine. As it evolved over time, each movement had meaning. Wiping the dirt and the rubber was a symbol of executing one pitch, clearing that pitch and then preparing for the next pitch. The breath was the last thing I did before I threw, and it was a symbol of trust and commitment to the present.

Earlier in my pitching career I did the same thing, but I hadn't yet attached the meaning to what I did. Once I added meaning to my routine it became a very valuable tool. It was the one thing I knew I had 100% control over. It allowed me to stay present and gave me clarity, especially in the times where everything surrounding me was in chaos.

We've all been there when we got sucked into our surroundings and before we knew it, it was out of control and seemed impossible to recover. For me it was the snowball effect of one mistake leading into several mistakes that eventually cost the team wins. For you it might have been in another arena when you allowed your surroundings to dictate your success. Circumstances that got you out of your routine, and when you finally recognized it, the damage had already been done.

Having a solid routine won't eliminate the chaos, but it allows you to stay under control so you have the ability to minimize potential damage. There is nothing better than watching someone remain calm while everything around them is hectic. When we see that, it helps simmer the fire and allows the emotions to subside. One person – that is all it takes. Most people look elsewhere for that person of reason to surface, but after you learn what a routine can do for you, that person everyone is looking for will be you.

The routine goes hand in hand with your goals, which will turn into your declaration, the power of perception and controlling the controllables. One of the things we have 100% control over is our routine. What do you do before you do it? Every time I say that, it sounds like something my ten-year-old son, Brayden, would say. Think about it, though. What do you do before you do it? How are you preparing for the moment? Are you flying by the seat of your pants or do you have a plan of attack? If you want control over your life, you need to prepare for everything you do, no matter how small it may seem. When you are the best, everything matters.

We all have a routine in our arena of competition, whether you know what it is or not. You have a routine in the weight room. You have a routine during practice. You have a routine while you're conditioning. Humans are creatures of habit, and this chapter will open your eyes to some of the things you can control to improve all aspects of life. You pretty much have a routine for everything you do and a lot of them you don't even think about.

What do you do when you get in a car? Put on a seatbelt.

What do you do before you go to bed? Shower, brush your teeth or some task to prepare for sleep. All routine.

Think about a typical day. You wake up, eat breakfast, go to school or work, come home and eat dinner, watch TV or do homework, go to bed and then repeat. I can almost guarantee you this generally sums up your day. If it does not, then I am giving you a virtual high five!!

What I want you to start thinking about are the specifics of your routine. Spend some time going over a day and notice the things that you consistently do. Might be scary to think about the majority of what we do as humans that we don't even pay attention to. What if we started paying attention to our actions and made sure they lined up with greatness? Now we are talking!! The best thing is we are not asking you to do the impossible. Just pay attention. As easy as it sounds, there are two things that will derail your train to awesome: *Emotions* and *Habits*. Let's identify these enemies.

It's pretty safe to say we can all look into our past to remember a moment when we reacted to something based on emotions. Said or did something that we regretted the moment we did it. We are constantly dealing with emotions and they are never going away. Think about the best in any arena and you will immediately see the sense of calm in their demeanor. Yes, they are emotional individuals, but they are in control of those emotions. That control of emotion is the difference that will take you to places even you did not think were possible.

Go back to what we talked about in the last chapter: emotions as waves. They come and they go. They are temporary. A particular emotion lasts about ninety seconds then goes away. That can seem like a lifetime when caught in the moment, but ride that wave of emotion and hold off reacting as long as you can. Once you are out of the emotion, it will be easier to make better choices. This will take some work, but by thinking of it you will see an immediate shift in the way you deal with situations. It is important to feel and understand that emotion. Don't give it power.

Habits are classified as good and bad. Remember the last time a parent, coach or supervisor told you to work on breaking those bad habits? WRONG! Why would you waste your time thinking about the things you don't do well? Once a habit is created it never goes away. As you waste your energy getting rid of something, you are losing precious time creating tools to help you achieve your dreams. Stop breaking bad habits and spend that time creating new and better ones. As you focus on the improved habit, it will override the bad one. It will take some time to create that habit, so stick with it for at least two weeks.

You see what we are doing here? Like I said earlier, we are not reinventing the wheel, just thinking differently. We are peeling the layers back to think bigger and play bigger. That's all. Nothing less, nothing more.

Back to routine.

Now that you are thinking about your routines, ask yourself if there is meaning to what you do. Why do you do it and how can you fine-tune it to make it better? It's that one thing that you go back to. You have all those uncontrollables that we talked about earlier surrounding you at all times. You have all those things that are potential distractions. The same thing that keeps most at bay from the top. Your routine will allow you to stay in the present. It allows you to get back to what you have the ability to control so you can execute.

All this is just a part of the process. You've got to be excited and have to start celebrating those little victories. You've got to start feeling good about the direction you're going. You've got to start thinking about your relationship with practice and how you can be better than anyone, because if you're prepared better than your competition, you're going to have the best chance to win no matter what arena you are in. If you pay attention to the little details, the small things, more than your competition, it's going to give you that edge.

Now that you have an idea of where we are going with routine, it is time to do some work. I love the question-and-answer portion because it allows you to think about how you can apply this to your daily routine. It adds clarity and sometimes reveals details you may not have come across if you just read.

Ready? If not, get ready and here we go.

Think about some physical routines you do daily, in meetings, in your athletic arena or where you spend most of your day. Or when you are most productive. For this exercise pick one or two to see the process.

What are some of your mental routines? What is the thought process in situations during your day? Do you see a pattern? Are they helping you or hurting you?

Why do you do the things you do in your physical and mental routines? Find a meaning with each action. If you can't find value or quality meaning, maybe it is not needed. As you think about this, ask yourself if these patterns have purpose. If you say *no* or can't find a reason, then they can probably be eliminated.

Answering the questions will give you clarity on a few routines, and then it is time to give it ownership. For you, where does your routine fit into the puzzle of peak performance? There has got to be an emotional investment. I do this because of this. I know I can go to my routine at any moment and it will get me right back to where I need to be. Having those thoughts attached to your routine will give it power. The deeper the meaning, the more power it possesses.

There is a fine line between routine and habit. In time you want to make your routine habit, but stay disciplined in the creation process to make sure every detail has meaning. That attention to detail makes your routine valuable and will be a powerful tool in any arena in your life.

I may be repeating myself, but I cannot express enough the importance of your relationship with practice, your passion for doing everything to the best of your ability. To not settle for "just enough" – and this applies to your routine. The best place to practice routine is during practice. I don't suggest bringing something new into a competitive environment until some comfort is attached to it. In time your routine will just happen, so make sure it is giving you what you need to be successful. There are also times where you just have to create something on the spot. The moment calls for something new and you just go! Make that decision, trust it, and then commit 100% to it. After it is over, you can evaluate and make adjustments if necessary. Some of our best memories are the moments that were not planned, they just happened. Embrace those with enthusiasm for the moment.

The proverbial road to the top is not going to be easy. As we add some tools to your arsenal, you will be prepared to handle the challenges constantly trying to break you down. When you are surrounded by chaos, go to your routine and it will get you back to what you can control. As you display a sense of control, it gives permission for others to do the same. You be the example. You be the standard-bearer.

Imagine you are in a high-pressure situation in a competitive arena. Everyone there knows the stakes are high and you can feel the tension in the air. Most of the people surrounding you are scared to fail. They hope they don't get the call to step up and be the hero. They would rather sit back and watch someone else do it. They would sacrifice the glory to not be the goat.

Then there is you. You feel the same pressure, but you also feel prepared for that moment. There is a sense of calm within you, and you block out all of the distractions getting in your way of shining in that moment. You don't wait to get the call; you take control and lead your team into the trenches, letting them know you got their back. They rally around you and you execute with grace, poise and purpose to victory.

Wow, that was kind of dreamy. That is what your life is going to be when you start living life with purpose. Not wandering around, hoping things will go your way. You get those moments in your life when your relationship with practice is intimate. When you stop labeling things as significant and non-significant. When everything you do matters.

Routine is just another piece of the puzzle. It has been in your life since the day you were born. Pretty safe to say that up until now, there was not a lot of thought to your routines and habits. Now that you have clarity on the power of them, start paying attention and making the necessary adjustments to create this amazing person that everyone wants to be around. There will be some setbacks because most of the people that surround you are not willing to do what you are doing. The more resistance you get, the better. It means you are on the right track.

Good idea to go back and think about your answers from the previous pages. Make sure they line up with where you are going. Once you feel good about them, understand and be OK with the fact that they will probably change. Not much, but as you change and get better at life, so will your routines. You are constantly evolving and if they just stay the same, they will no longer have the significance they need to have. Just a heads-up. It will happen. Another sign that you are awesome!

# RECONNECTING TO THE BREATH

---

Take a good deep breath. Don't put a lot of thought into it. Just do whatever comes naturally to you.

Now take another deep breath, but this time I want you to pay attention to a few things. Are your shoulders rising as you inhale? Do your chest, stomach or both expand as you inhale? Is your exhale short or long?

A little different than the first breath?

Now I want you to take a breath as you inhale through your nose. Put your hand on the bottom of your rib cage and let everything below that expand during your inhale. Fill your stomach with as much air as possible, and once you reach your capacity, hold it for two or three seconds. As you exhale, open your mouth and let all the air out; and if there are people around you, I want them to hear you exhale. Who cares what ink? I know you were thinking about what may say or think about you. Who cares?

Now that is a quality breath. How did you feel after taking that last breath? For me, it instantly grounds me and gets me present. If that was not the feeling you had, then try it one more time with the intention of being present.

Another great example of a quality breath is watching an infant sleep. Notice how the breath is controlled and how the stomach rises and falls with each breath.

You might think to yourself, *a whole chapter on the breath?* When I got my master's in Sports Psychology, I did my whole thesis on breathing – some proper ways of breathing and why we have lost our connection with the breath.

The breath is the one tool that we've had since the day we were born and it's the last thing we're going to do before we pass. This may be the most important chapter in this book, and when you reconnect with your breath, it will become your biggest asset.

Why have we lost connection? Let's go back to watching an infant breathe. It's a slow, controlled breath. The belly expands with each inhale and goes back down with each exhale.

As we get older, we start breathing in our chest. Our shoulders rise and typically our adult breath is quick and short. At what point do we lose that valuable connection with our breath? Gets you thinking, right? Just by reading this you are paying attention to how you breathe. Mission accomplished... I can stop now. But I won't because there is more to say.

It is my belief that our breath changes because as we get older we lose the ability to stay present. When you are an infant, toddler or even an adolescent there are not a lot of things to worry about. Life is simple and the few things that consume their mind are typically what they are doing NOW. They are present!

With age comes responsibility and too many options. Yes, I said it: too many options. Most people think having all these options is great. They confuse us and we never commit to anything because we want to "keep our options open."

Let's face it. We are an anxious society. We are typically stressed and unhappy. Brutal but true. The rat race of life has us going in so many different directions and we never take the time to be present and enjoy what's happening. It is all about what happened or what may happen. NO CONTROL! This is just my opinion, but if we would actually slow down a bit and eliminate options, we would be more present and our natural breathing patterns would return. It would also take some practice to create a new habit of taking good deep breaths.

Let's think about this for a moment. Go back to the last time you were put into a stressful situation or fear shows up. What happens? The breath gets quick and short. The heart rate increases and you start sweating. Some go as far as hyperventilating. It is not a good feeling. What happens next is you try to get out of that environment or situation as fast as possible. Fight or flight takes over. You begin to rush and you no longer have any control over the situation. Things get really fast and you are flooded with emotions. It happens to all of us and will probably happen again in the near future – in an athletic arena, business meeting or asking someone out on a date. All hell breaks loose!! No fight, all flight! You are out or want out as fast as possible. Here is what I want you to think about. You cannot control some of the environments or situations that you get put into, but you can control how you react to those moments.

Imagine the next time you get into one of those moments. It probably will happen sooner than you would like. This time you take a good deep breath. That breath will get you present and allow you to make better choices. Those choices will give you a better chance of making any moment a better moment. Possibly still not an enjoyable moment, but by taking some of the emotions out of the situation, you will be the person of reason. That is a skill that will separate you from most in the environment you are in. That makes you the person people go to when chaos surrounds you. That makes you a great leader. All because you have the ability to recognize the environment, take that quality breath, and act accordingly.

I do this drill with a lot of people that I work with and I want you to do this on your own. Get a stopwatch and breathe as fast as you can, inhale and exhale as fast as you can, for 30 seconds. When you are done, feel your heart rate. Pay attention to how you feel. That's pressure, stress and anxiety – all the stuff we pile on top of ourselves on a daily basis.

Now take a real good, deep inhale for a five or six count, hold it for a two count and exhale for a 7 or 8 count. Watch how quick your heart rate goes down; watch how quick you to get back into the present moment. Powerful, right?

With your breath in mind, spend a few moments thinking about these questions and try to apply what you have learned in this chapter to your daily routine. When we started this journey we began with the plan, talked about our perception, what we can control, and routine. Now the breath will allow us to be present to chip away at that plan, and before you know it you are full steam ahead to greatness.

When you are under pressure, have adversity or experience failure, how are your breath and heart rates? It's kind of an obvious question, but I want you to think about some details during those situations. Heart rate increases with adversity, perceived pressure and anxiety. Ask yourself why this happens? I will give my thoughts on that in a minute.

When you're under pressure, what are the feelings you experience? Does it feel like your heart is pounding out of your chest? Can you feel yourself with the short, quick breaths? Can you not think clearly? Just reliving a moment can sometimes trigger the same feelings.

Do you ever think about your breath while competing in whatever arena you're in? Do you have a connection with your breath? I mean, we've done it since the day we were born; we're going to do it until the day we die. Most of the time we take the breath for granted. What does it mean to reconnect? What would it mean to think about breathing the proper way? Hopefully you've already gotten that feeling because we've introduced it and you've started to think about it. Once you start thinking about it, you're going to tend to do it properly. As we have that thought process of, "Am I breathing the right way?" you're going to breathe the right way and it's creating new habits.

Where does the breath fit in your routine, or do you already have a breath as part of your routine? If a good deep breath is not in your routine, find a way to add it in. For me it was the last thing I did before I took action. Before speaking at an event, the last thing I would do before going on stage was take a good deep breath. Before a big meeting. Before the big game. Before you ask her out on a date. Deep breath, and go get it.

Think of some times and places where you can use the breath as a tool to give you the best chance for success. As you learn these tools, we've talked about perception, we've talked about controlling the controllables and a routine, and we now have some specific goals set. As you start applying these to practice and as they start to become part of your habits, you're going to feel less anxiety and you're going to feel less pressure or potential fear as you perform – but when you do have those moments, where can you use the breath?

It's paying attention to your breath before it gets out of hand, but also recognizing when you're not where you need to be. Take that good deep breath and get back into the present moment. I also think you can anticipate a potential tough situation and prepare yourself. When you are prepared, you have a better sense of knowing if you are in a good frame of mind. Half the battle is knowing you are not where you need to be.

Understanding where you are allows you to adjust when necessary.

You've got to have positive self-talk. You need to know you got this. I got this, I'm going to do this, I'm going to commit to this 100% and if I fail, I will have no regrets. If you do that more times than not, you're going to get the results you want. You need to focus on the process. Part of the process is understanding, knowing and having a relationship with proper breathing.

As you grind through your day, check in with yourself several times. How is my breathing? Am I present right now? Am I working on my dreams? Just doing that locks you in and gives you that sense of calmness and clarity, which allows you to make better choices. Those choices give you the best chance for success.

Action steps! It all comes down to action. You now have some knowledge about reconnecting with your breath. What are you going to do to stay connected? What are you going to do to create new habits with your breathing?

The breath is a tool that allows you to be present more often. Keeps you focused on the task at hand. The ability to think, to make better choices, and all these things stacked up are really going to give you that chance to be the best version of yourself. It's not guaranteed, we know that, but it's part of the process. It's part of the grind. It's necessary to increase your relationship with practice.

We've set our foundation and now it's the details on a daily basis over a consistent amount of time that creates everything you want. Don't ever lose the details. The simplest thing is what gives you the foundation to be the best of the best, where there is no competition.

As we wrap this chapter up, I want you to understand how important the breath is. When you take a good, deep breath, it gets you present. It allows you to stay calm and make quality choices. I am sure you have heard that too many times and I do not want to beat a dead horse, so I will leave it at that.

As you go about your day, just pay attention to your breath. If you have time, start your day with just you and your breath. It really prepares you for the craziness of life. We are not going to avoid all the crap life throws at us. I don't want that. I think the pain, failures and struggles are necessary to be the best. I am just arming you with you some tools to keep those moments short. Even learn from them to prepare you for the next opportunity.

# RELAXATION AND VISUALIZATION

This is the last chapter of *The Mental Locker*. It is my hope that it has been a good read and you captured a few nuggets that you will apply to your life immediately. This has been an amazing journey for me, telling my stories and reliving some of the most vivid memories I have.

As you continue to take action and apply these tools to your everyday practice, you will rise to the top. It's just a matter of time. You've got to be patient. You've got to keep pushing your boundaries. You've got to keep shattering your expectations of what you think you are capable of becoming. You've got to be comfortable being uncomfortable. That's a lot of *you've gots*, but if you have gotten this far in the book, you understand where you are going and have some clarity on how to get there.

This was and still is the hardest part for me. When I want something, I want it now. I am sure you feel the same way. Do what you have to do and remind yourself that anything worth having takes time to get. Run the miles, and before you know it all of your dreams will be right in front of you and the people you respect the most will surround you.

Relaxation and Visualization – I love this one. I know every chapter I get to, it's like, "This is my favorite one! No, this is my favorite one." Breathing for me is the number one tool, and that leads right into relaxation and visualization.

Quick reminder: The mind does not know the difference between perception and reality. It is scientifically proven that if we lie down in a bed and visualize physical activity, we fire the same muscles in our brain and stimulate the same muscles in our body that we actually do when we do it physically. Obviously, you're going to get stronger by physically doing it. The point is, as we learn to visualize success or even overcoming failure, we are training our body and mind to be the best.

As you attack your plan and turn it into your declaration, you now have these tools to help you through the process. They will be your fighting force when all the distraction and pain come to knock you off track. Believe me, that time is coming, but when you prepare for it, you have a chance.

I want you to start developing a relationship with your future self. Everything you do from this day forward MUST line up with your future self. If it is not leading to being THE BEST, you need to eliminate it. I know that sounds cold, but it has to happen to get to where you want to go. To be the best you must be willing to eliminate everything in your life that is not excellent. That's how it has to be.

Imagine what your life would look like if you went about your day with only one thing on your mind and that was to be the best. It really simplifies everything. Is this helping me or hurting me? Simple question with a simple *yes* or *no* answer. If yes, keep moving. If not, adjust and keep moving.

When you visualize how you're going to be the best, you will become very familiar with whom you need to become. What does he or she look like? How does he or she act? What is his/her daily practice? See this using all of your senses and make it as real as possible. This cannot be a once-in-a-while thing. It has to be an everyday thing. That consistency will put you in a good frame of mind and those visions will become your reality. In time you will live right into your vision.

With that said, this should come with a warning label. Be careful what you visualize. Be careful for what you manifest into your world. Are you ready for greatness? Are you ready to become the future self that you have designed? Of course you are, but you have to trust that so it can happen. It's already done; you just have to put the work into it. Run the miles to collide with your destiny.

Back to the commitment of the daily practice of visualization. Even if it's for five minutes a day. I'm sure you could find five minutes a day to do some visualization on seeing yourself, feeling yourself, hearing yourself in successful situations. Even overcoming failure. Remember failure is never going away, but if we see it as a tool for success, we can deal with it as a productive part of the process. We don't want to accept failure, but we have to know that it is a part of being the best. Being successful, feeling what it's like to be the best. Five minutes a day — if you take that time and add it up over weeks, months, potentially years, there is no competition; it's as simple as that.

Here is a basic outline of a visualization session. The key is to relax and spend some time with you. I like to sit or lie in a quiet place and listen to some soft music. Music can be optional. I focus on my breath and get as present as I can. There will be thoughts and distractions, and that is OK. Recognize if your mind is wandering and come back to the breath.

Once I am present and grounded, I begin a process of tightening and relaxing my muscles. Start with your feet and work your way up to the head. Feet, ankles, calves, hamstrings, quads, abs, chest, shoulders, arms, neck and back. Basically run a check on your entire body. I like to end with the head because that is where all the power lies – our thoughts. The only thought is releasing tension and allowing the ground to take your body's weight.

Once I am done with the body scan, I will go back and revisit any areas that may need a little more attention. Could be a sore part of the body and just some built-up tension in the shoulders or lower back area.

Once your body is relaxed you can start visualizing.

There are two types of visualization: internal and external.

Internal is feeling during visualization. Seeing it through your own eyes. Re-creating or preparing for moments as if you are actually doing it.
External is when you are watching yourself. You're sitting in the stands or on the sidelines

watching yourself perform and seeing the details of it.

So which one are you better at? Let's say you find yourself more internal than external. I want you to work on the external, and vice versa.

We always want to work on our weaknesses and maintain our strengths. A lot of times we want to go right to our strengths because that's where we are comfortable. We don't want to be comfortable; we want to be uncomfortable because we're pushing our boundaries. Get an idea of where you're at internally or externally when it comes to visualization. Try to get great at both; that happens with practice, just like anything else we want to be great at.

When you visualize, engage all senses. See, feel, smell, taste and touch what you are seeing. The more realistic you make it, the quicker it becomes your reality. In time you will be a pro at this, and you know you are in the right place when you are practicing visualization and you actually forget it was just in your mind. It's like waking up from a dream and asking yourself if that really happened. A little freaky but cool at the same time. This is such a powerful skill and so many elite people talk about how they saw themselves at a certain level way before they got there. If you see it and believe it, your mind will guide you in the right direction.

Are you internal or external? Do you see negatives? Do you see positives? Can you engage all the senses or is it difficult? Once you get that foundation, you have an idea of where you're going to go from there. The key is to start and then focus on the daily practice. Stick with it for a few weeks no matter how frustrating it gets. If you just sit and focus on your breath for five minutes, that is progress.

You have heard it once, maybe twice, but here we go again. The mind doesn't know the difference between perception and reality. You've got to understand that. That is why your thoughts, self-talk and the noise that surrounds you matter. They create your reality. Don't like where you are? Change. Stop blaming everyone

for where you are and do something abou̅
it matters enough and you care enough, you wii̅
do whatever it takes to get there. Seeing it first
allows you to familiarize yourself with what will
be.

This is the final step; the final tool to get you to
the top of your game is seeing yourself do it over
and over. Don't mistake this for a finish line. If
you want an arrival point, you will not find one
here. The work has just begun. Isn't that
refreshing to know that for the rest of your life
you will work on being the best you and nothing
else? Simplifies what you do on a daily basis.

What you've received in *The Mental Locker* are
tools to go to battle with. Now it is up to you to
use them or disregard them. If you choose to
fight for what you want, you will bleed, cry, fail,
be lonely at times and experience pain. It will be
worth it. You will look back at your journey and
be proud of the legacy you have created. When
your fight ends, someone you have inspired will
pick up the torch and continue the fight for you.
This will go on for generations and the world will

be a better place because you made the simple decision to fight. When you made that decision, you gave other people permission to make the same decision.

If you choose not to fight, nothing will change. You will reduce yourself to the norm, and for some people that is OK with them. I have no interest in that, and if I am a betting man, neither are you. If you were someone who likes to fit in and settles for just enough, you would not have made it this far. For that I say *Congratulations!* You have just joined the minority in fighting for something BIG.

Here are some things to chew on when it comes to relaxation and visualization.

When you're tense, where do you feel it most? When experiencing stress, pressure and anxiety, where do you feel the tension? For me it was always in my shoulders. When I learned to relax, it really changed things.

As you find out where you carry your tension, ask yourself a few questions. Can I control why I am feeling the way I am feeling? How can I see this situation in a different way? A lot of times asking these questions reduces the tension. Now take some time to relax and focus on the areas you have identified.

When the game is on the line, you are about to enter a big meeting or are having an intense conversation with your parents, describe your emotions. Are you nervous? Are you scared? Do you want to get it over as quick as you can? How do you deal with your nervous energy? Is it helping you or hurting you in that situation? I know – too many questions.

When you visualize, how clear is it? Are you engaging all your senses? Can you smell, feel and taste? Be specific on where you're at with your details when you visualize.

Are you comfortable with internal or external?

When can you use visualization and relaxation to give you the best chance for success? We talked about this in the last question. This is not the night before kind of thing. This is a daily ritual, a daily routine. Some people like to do it again right before they perform and some the night before. Is there a specific time during your day where you feel you're more engaged with the relaxation and visualization? It may vary, but that's why we're doing this. I want you to find some specific details.

How will you apply it every day? It becomes a part of your relationship with practice. It becomes a part of your daily routine, your daily grind.

You've heard me say that a bunch of times, and it all comes down to doing more, paying attention to the details, doing the little things over a significant period of time.

It's not this huge drastic overhaul; it's the basics. Pulling back and really locking in on the details of what it takes to be the best. Not just good, not just whatever everyone else does – that's not good enough for us. It doesn't mean longer; it means better, more efficient, working smart versus working hard. Do you know the difference?

You must take massive action every day. Every single day you're working toward greatness. Working on your controllables, your perception, your plan, daily routine, the breath and relaxation and visualization. Then it's a matter of trusting them as you grind your way into the best version of who you are.

As we wrap a bow around this project, I want to thank you for spending some time with me. You have given me the opportunity to share my experiences with you and I take that responsibility seriously. They've worked for me and I know they're going to work for you if you take action. I have loved this process of giving you all I have.

As you interpret *The Mental Locker* and the tools that we have provided, take pride in embedding it into your molecules. Start sharing it with people and be prepared for people to line up to help you get to where you want to go. If you don't tell people where you are going, how are they supposed to help? They want to be a part of something bigger than themselves, and amazing people and opportunities will come your way the more you express who you will become.

These skills I have so much passion for allowed me to achieve things I never thought possible. It has allowed me to be things I never even thought about. It has allowed me to be a good coach, father, husband and to influence people in ways words cannot explain. Greatness begins to show up everywhere and continues to fuel the fire within.

Take your experiences and share them, embrace them, and give others permission to play a bigger game in life.

As you begin to separate yourself from most people, they're going to look at you in a different way. You may begin to hear things like "This

guy's on his own program; who does h
is?" Doesn't matter. Continue to go o
to greatness and anyone who doesn
follow you, leave them behind. Better yet, they
will dismiss themselves from your life and find
somewhere else to "fit in." Boring!!

Grab some of the people that want to go with
you, to be elite, to be on top. That's the only
place to be, but it's hard to get there. It's painful;
it's filled with sweat, blood, tears, and
exhaustion. But when you're there, it feels
amazing!

Be careful as you rise to the top. We see it all the
time with elite athletes. They look down on
people as if they are better than them or
accomplished more than them. That is ego;
beware of it.

Grab the right people and let them see the view
from the top, because it looks good. You're
becoming elite, the best, but you need to remind
yourself it's a process. It's not a short-term thing
and as you grow, you've got to keep pushing,

u've got to keep pushing, and you've got to keep pushing. Did I mention push? Before you know it your Untouchable Goals will be right in front of your face.

Visualize your success, the details of what it takes to be the best, and don't stop. Keep pushing, keep grinding, and love every minute of it.

Your relationship with practice, your relationship with pain – and you're going to have to sacrifice. I'm telling you, it's not easy, but you now have the tools to be successful. You now have the tools to get to the highest level, whatever that is for you. You have the physical and the mental tools. Time to marry them together and play the hardest game you know how to play. Don't stop until you get what you want, and when you get it, keep going. You keep going until you take your last breath on earth. Now that's living a good life!

I want to end this like I end all my speeches. My daughter Hailey is thirteen and she is a dancer.

Poetry in motion, and the letter below is a letter from Martha Graham to one of her students. Martha Graham is the best choreographer of all time and I leave her words with you...

# A Letter to Agnes de Mille

There is a vitality,
a life force,
a quickening
that is translated through you into action,
and because there is only one of you in all time,
this expression is unique.

And if you block it, it will never exist through any other
medium and be lost.
The world will not have it. It is not your business to determine
how good it is
nor how valuable it is
nor how it compares with other expressions.

It is your business to keep it yours clearly and directly
to keep the channel open.
You do not even have to believe in yourself or your work.
You have to keep open and aware directly to the urges that
motivate YOU.

Keep the channel open...
No artist is pleased...

There is no satisfaction whatever at any time.
There is only a queer, divine dissatisfaction,
a blessed unrest that keeps us marching
and makes "us" MORE alive than the others.

-Martha Graham

Made in the USA
Middletown, DE
14 January 2017